AF234914

Impressum
Verlag: BABADADA GmbH, Nedderfeld 112 , 22529 Hamburg
Geschäftsführer / Verlagsleitung: Harald Hof
Druck: Books on Demand GmbH, In de Tarpen 42, 22848 Norderstedt

Imprint
Publisher: BABADADA GmbH, Nedderfeld 112 , 22529 Hamburg, Germany
Managing Director / Publishing direction: Harald Hof
Print: Books on Demand GmbH, In de Tarpen 42, 22848 Norderstedt

škola

school

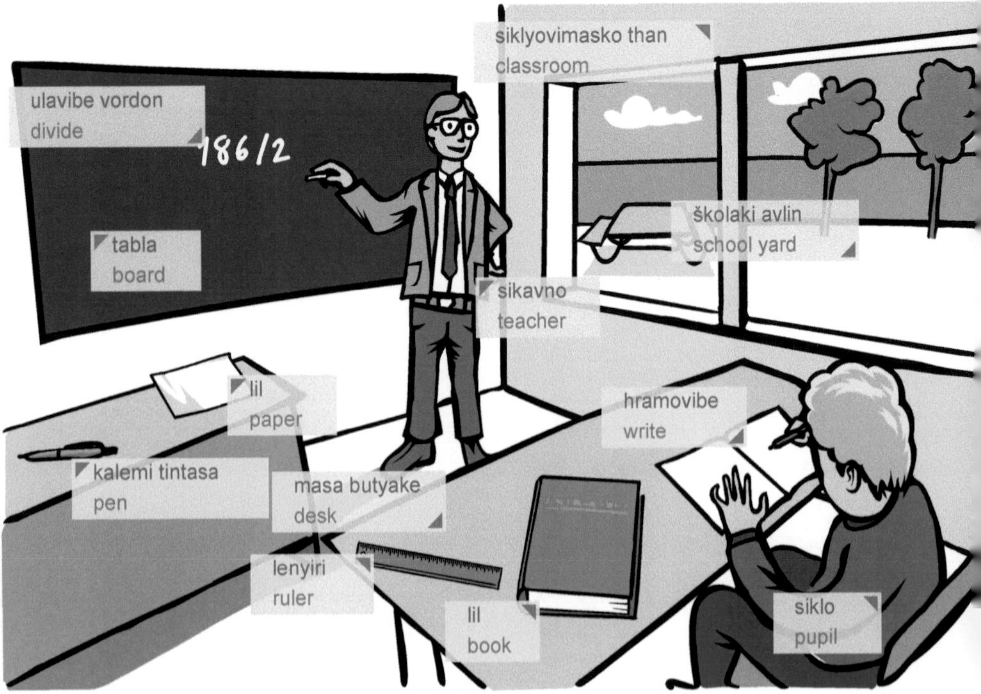
siklyovimasko than
classroom
ulavibe vordon
divide
186/2
tabla
board
školaki avlin
school yard
sikavno
teacher
lil
paper
hramovibe
write
kalemi tintasa
pen
masa butyake
desk
lenyiri
ruler
lil
book
siklo
pupil

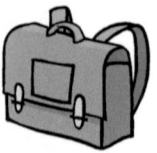

dumeski tašna

satchel

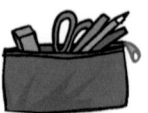

kalemengi kutia

pencil case

kalemi

pencil

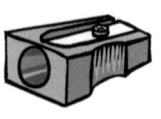

kalemengi čhurori

pencil sharpener

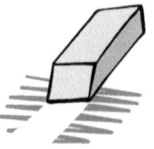

kosimaski guma

rubber

čitrimasko bloko

drawing pad

čitribe

drawing

boyimaski frča

paintbrush

boyimaski kutia

paint box

kata

scissors

lepako

glue

bukjardarimasko lil

exercise book

khereski buti

homework

gendo

number

džide

add

ikal

subtract

multiplicirin

multiply

kalkulirin

calculate

hramome lil

letter

alfabeta

alphabet

lafo

word

teksti

text

drabaribe

read

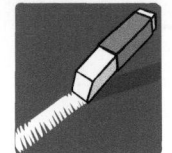

kreda

chalk

lekciya

lesson

Klasesko registro

register

egzameni

exam

sertifikato

certificate

školaki uniforma

school uniform

edukacia

education

enciklopedia

encyclopedia

univerziteto

university

mikroskopo

microscope

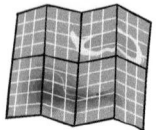

mapa

map

korpa čhudimaske lila

waste-paper basket

4

škola - school

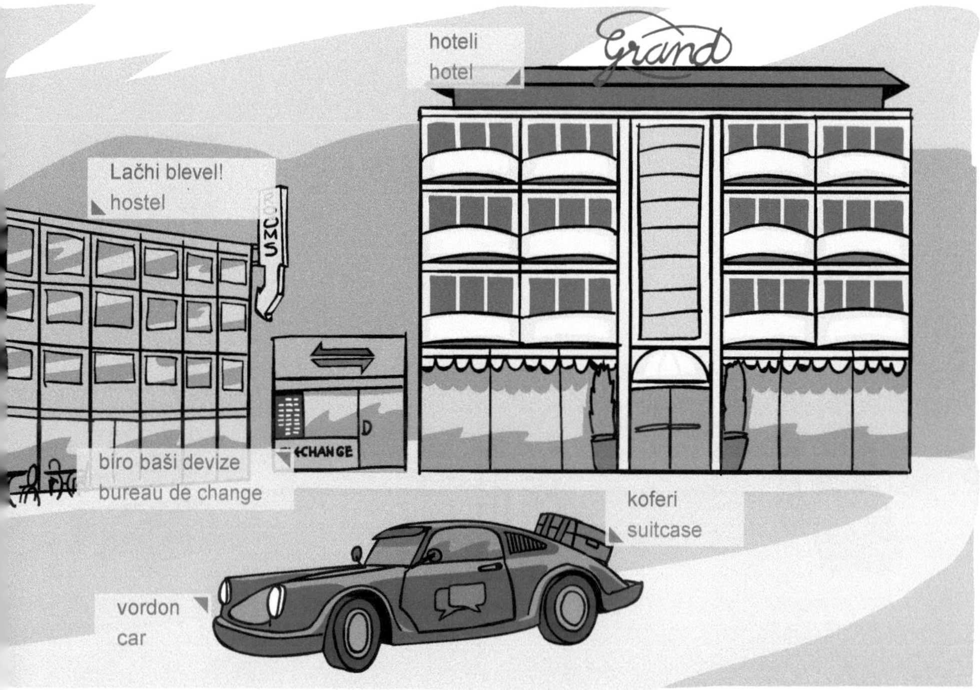

hoteli
hotel
Grand
Lačhi blevel!
hostel
ROOMS
biro baši devize
bureau de change
CHANGE
koferi
suitcase
vordon
car

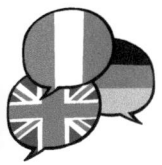

ćhib
language

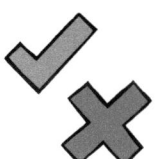

va / na
yes / no

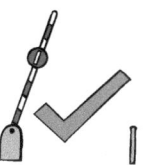

Okay
Okay

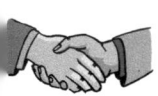

Namaste
hello

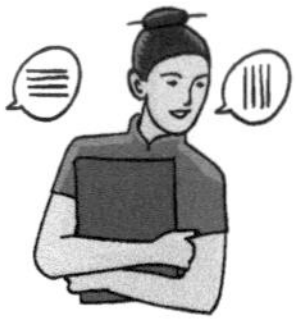

tumači
translator

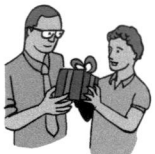

Ov sasto
Thank you

Kozom si...?

how much is...?

Na havava

I do not understand

problemo

problem

Lačhi rat!

Good evening!

Lačhi javin!

Good morning!

Lačhi rat!

Good night!

ačhon Devlesa

bye bye

dromeski sikavin

direction

bagaži

luggage

gono

bag

dumesko gono

backpack

misafiri

guest

kamara

room

sovimasko gono

sleeping bag

cerha

tent

ristikani informacia

tourist information

plaža

beach

kreditno kartica

credit card

javinako habe

breakfast

kušluko

lunch

ratyako habe

dinner

karta

ticket

elevatori

lift

marka

stamp

simantra

border

adetia

customs

ambasada

embassy

viza

visa

pašaporti

passport

transporti

transport

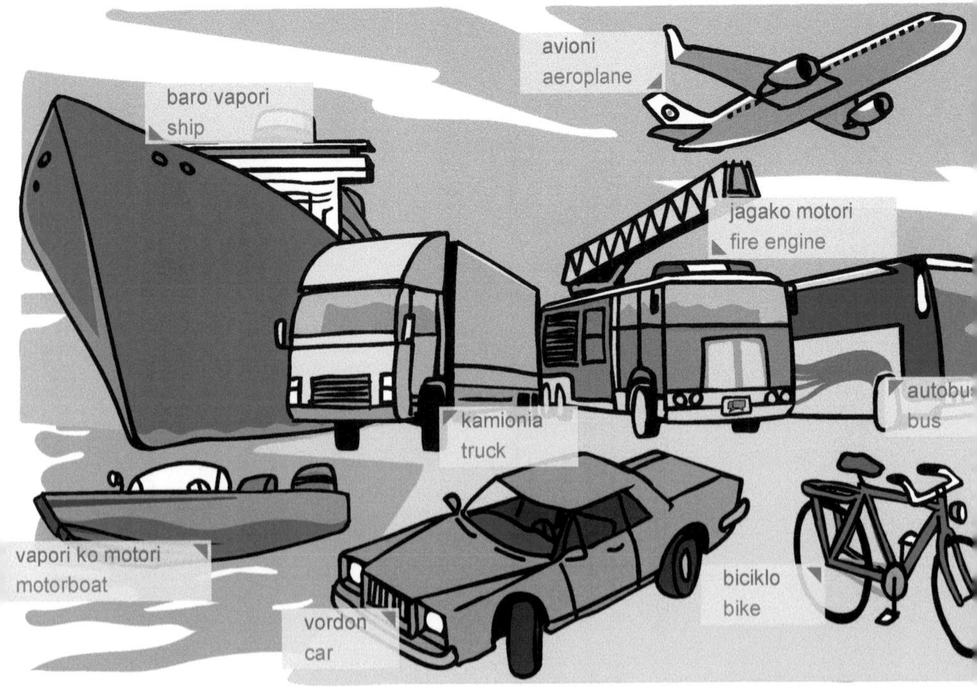
avioni
aeroplane
baro vapori
ship
jagako motori
fire engine
autobu
bus
kamionia
truck
vapori ko motori
motorboat
biciklo
bike
vordon
car

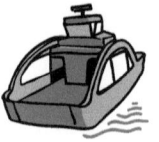

feri vapori

ferry

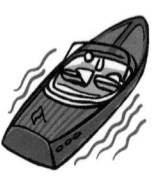

vapori

boat

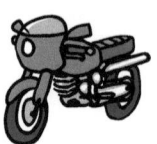

motorciklo

motorbike

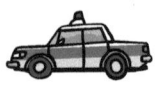

policiako vordon

police car

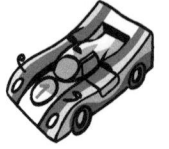

prastamasko vordon

racing car

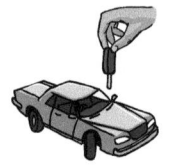

rentakar

rental car

ulavibe vordon

car sharing

rumosardo kamioni

breakdown truck

kamionengo than

refuse truck

motori

motor

petroli

fuel

petrolesko stasioni

petrol station

afikoskere išaretia

traffic sign

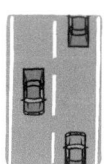

trafiko

traffic

baro trafiko

traffic jam

onesko parkirimasko than

car park

pampurengo stasioni

train station

kamionia

tracks

pampuri

train

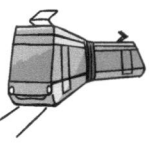

tramvaj

tram

vagoni

carriage

helikopteri

helicopter

aeroporti

airport

kula

tower

dromarutno

passenger

kontejneri

container

kartoni

carton

vordonoro

cart

sevli

basket

urjalipasko starto /
urjalipasko agor

take off / land

diz
city

gav

village

dizyako centro

city centre

kher

house

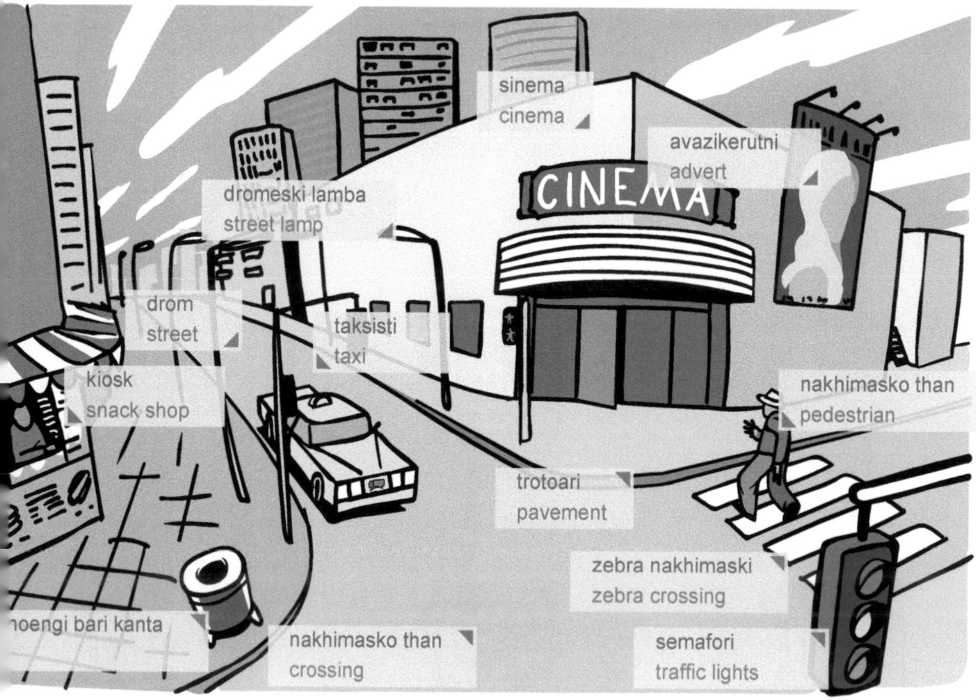

sinema
cinema

avazikerutni
advert

dromeski lamba
street lamp

CINEMA

drom
street

taksisti
taxi

kiosk
snack shop

nakhimasko than
pedestrian

trotoari
pavement

zebra nakhimaski
zebra crossing

noengi bari kanta

nakhimasko than
crossing

semafori
traffic lights

koliba

hut

apartmani

flat

pampurengo stasioni

train station

dizyaki sala

town hall

muzeji

museum

škola

school

univerziteto
university

banka
bank

hospitalo
hospital

hoteli
hotel

apoteka
pharmacy

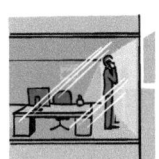

ofiso
office

lil bikinimasko than
book shop

dukyano
shop

lulugengo bikinutno
florist's

supermarket
supermarket

kurko
market

baro bikinimasko kher
department store

mačhengo astarutno
fishmonger's

kinimasko centro
shopping centre

vaporengo ačhovimasko than
harbour

parko

park

klupa

bench

purt

bridge

merdevenya

stairs

metro stasioni

underground

tuneli

tunnel

tobuseski adžikerin

bus stop

bar

bar

restorani

restaurant

poštako mohto

postbox

dromesko išareti

street sign

parking than

parking meter

zoo

zoo

nangyovimasko bazeni

swimming pool

džamiya

mosque

farma
....
farm

melalipe
....
pollution

limorengo than
....
graveyard

khangeri
....
church

khelimasko than
....
playground

hramo
....
temple

pejzaži
landscape

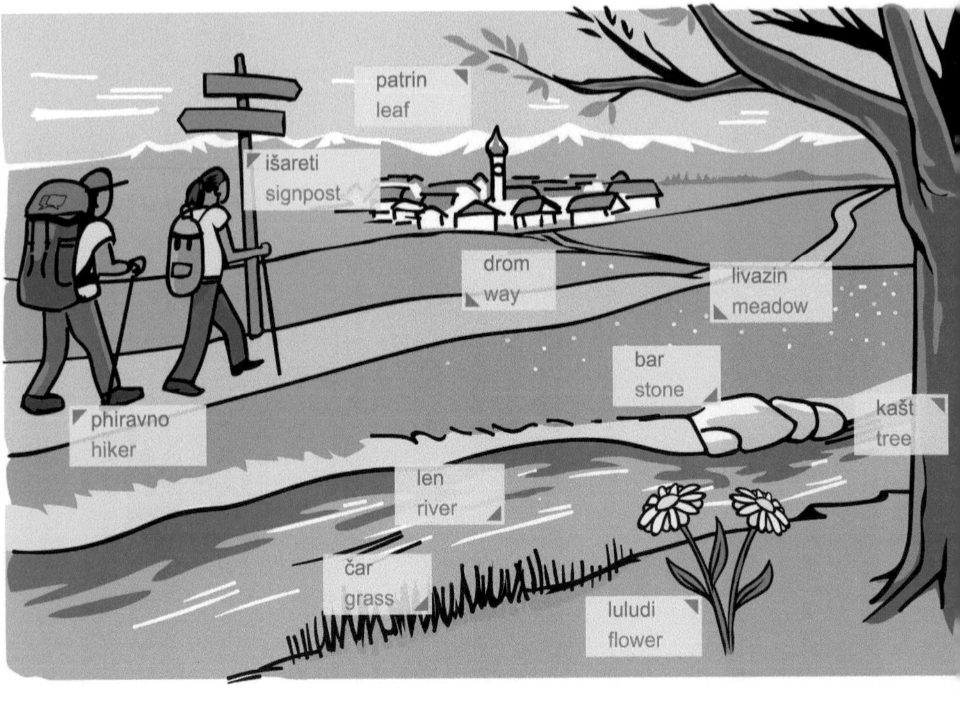

patrin
leaf

išareti
signpost

drom
way

livazin
meadow

bar
stone

kašt
tree

phiravno
hiker

len
river

čar
grass

luludi
flower

harno than

valley

bairi

hill

devrijal

lake

veš

forest

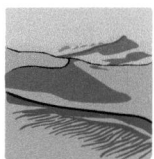

mulano than

desert

vulkano

volcano

saraji

castle

renkali badalin

rainbow

gaba

mushroom

palma kašt

palm tree

sivrija

mosquito

mak

fly

karandža

ant

birumni

bee

pauko

spider

buba

beetle

žamba

frog

ververica

squirrel

kanzauri

hedgehog

šošoj

hare

buf

owl

pakšin

bird

lebedi

swan

bali

boar

eleno

deer

eleno

moose

pani garavin

dam

bavlalaki turbina

wind turbine

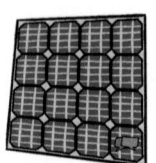

solarno paneli

solar panel

klima

climate

restorani
restaurant

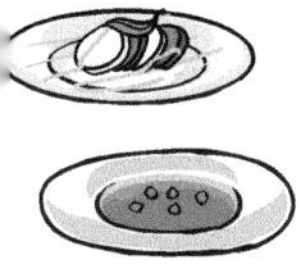

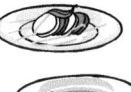

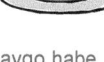

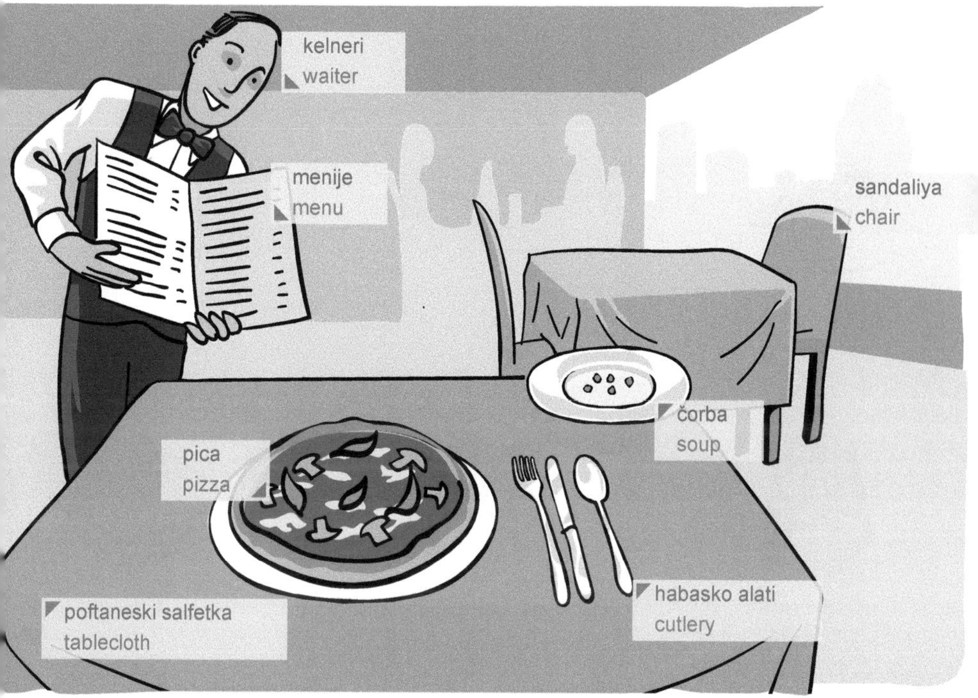

kelneri
waiter
menije
menu
sandaliya
chair
čorba
soup
pica
pizza
habasko alati
cutlery
poftaneski salfetka
tablecloth

avgo habe

starter

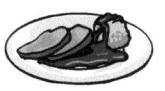

šerutno habe

main course

gudlimata

dessert

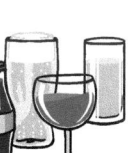

piiba

drinks

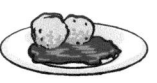

habe

food

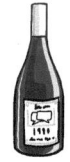

šiša

bottle

fast food

fast food

sokakongo habe

street food

čajniko

teapot

šekereskoro čaroro

sugar bowl

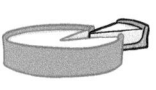

porcia

portion

makina vaš espresso

espresso machine

uči sandaliya

high chair

esapi

bill

apladiya

tray

čhuri

knife

vilyuška

fork

roj

spoon

čajeski roj

teaspoon

salfetka

serviette

tahtai

glass

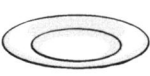

čaro
....
plate

čaro čorbake
....
soup plate

hor čaro
....
saucer

sosi
....
sauce

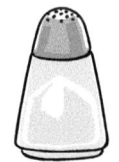

londesko čaroro
....
salt pot

kale biberesko pišlo
....
pepper mill

šut
....
vinegar

zejtini
....
oil

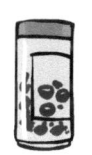

začinia
....
spices

kečap
....
ketchup

senf
....
mustard

majonezi
....
mayonnaise

supermarket

supermarket

specialno oferta
special offer
FOR
mušteriya
customer
thudeske butya
dairy
emiši
fruit
vordonoro
trolley

BUTCHERS

kasapi

butcher´s

BAKERY

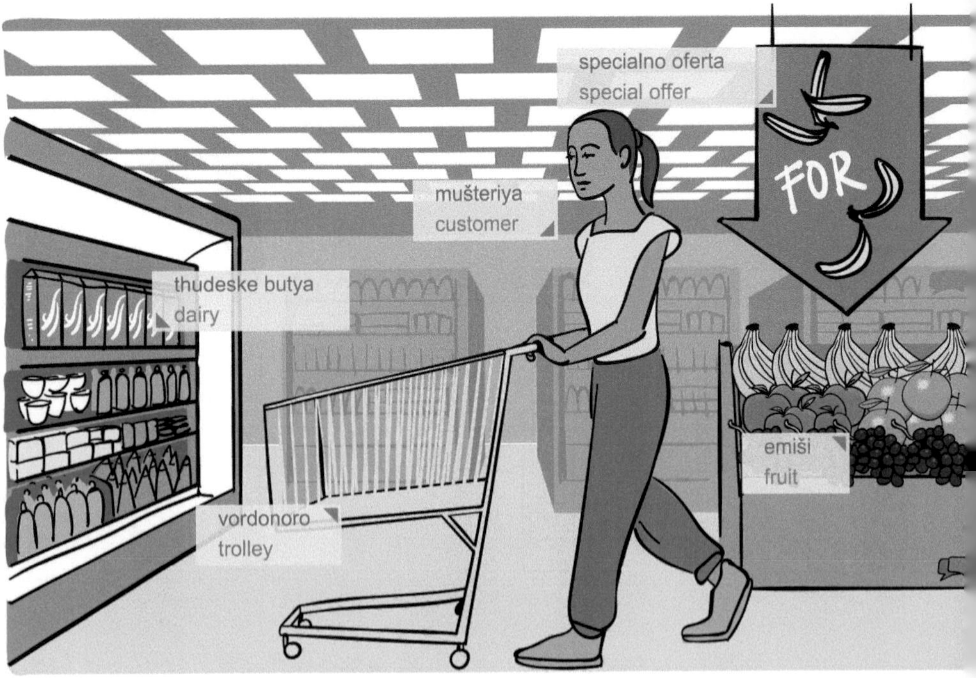

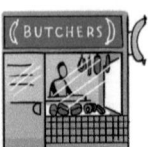

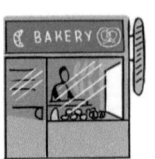

furuna

baker´s

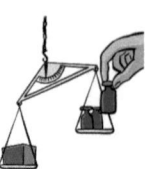

ladavipe

weigh

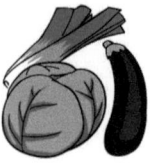

zarzavati

vegetables

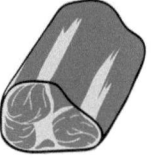

masesko rolati

meat

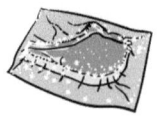

pahome habe

frozen food

šudro mas

cold meat

konzerva

tinned food

thovimasko prašako

washing powder

gudlimata

sweets

khereske butya

household products

užarimaske butya

cleaning products

bikinutno

salesperson

kasapi

till

kasieri

cashier

kinimaski patrin

shopping list

putarimaske satura

opening hours

lovengi tašna

wallet

kreditno kartica

credit card

gono

bag

plastikano gono

plastic bag

pani

water

džus

juice

thud

milk

kola

coke

mol

wine

bira

beer

alkohol

alcohol

kakao

cocoa

čaj

tea

kafa

coffee

espresso

espresso

cappuccino

cappuccino

banana

banana

phabaj

apple

portokali

orange

kavuni

melon

limoni

lemon

karota

carrot

sir

garlic

bambusi

bamboo

purum

onion

gaba

mushroom

akhora

nuts

humereske butya

noodles

špageti

spaghetti

rezo

rice

salata

salad

čipsi

chips

peke kompiria

fried potatoes

pica

pizza

hamburger

hamburger

sendviči

sandwich

kotleti

cutlet

žamboni

ham

salama

salami

goja

sausage

khajnako mas

chicken

peko

roast

mačho

fish

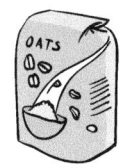

popara

porridge oats

musli

muesli

kornfleks

cornflakes

varo

flour

kroasani

croissant

masesko rolati

bread roll

maro

bread

tosti

toast

biskotia

biscuits

puteri

butter

urda

curd

torta

cake

jaro

egg

peke jare

fried egg

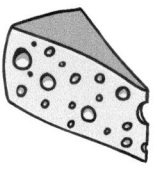

kiral

cheese

šudro gudlo

ice cream

šekeri

sugar

avgin

honey

džem

jam

čokoladaki krema

chocolate spread

kari

curry

farma
farm

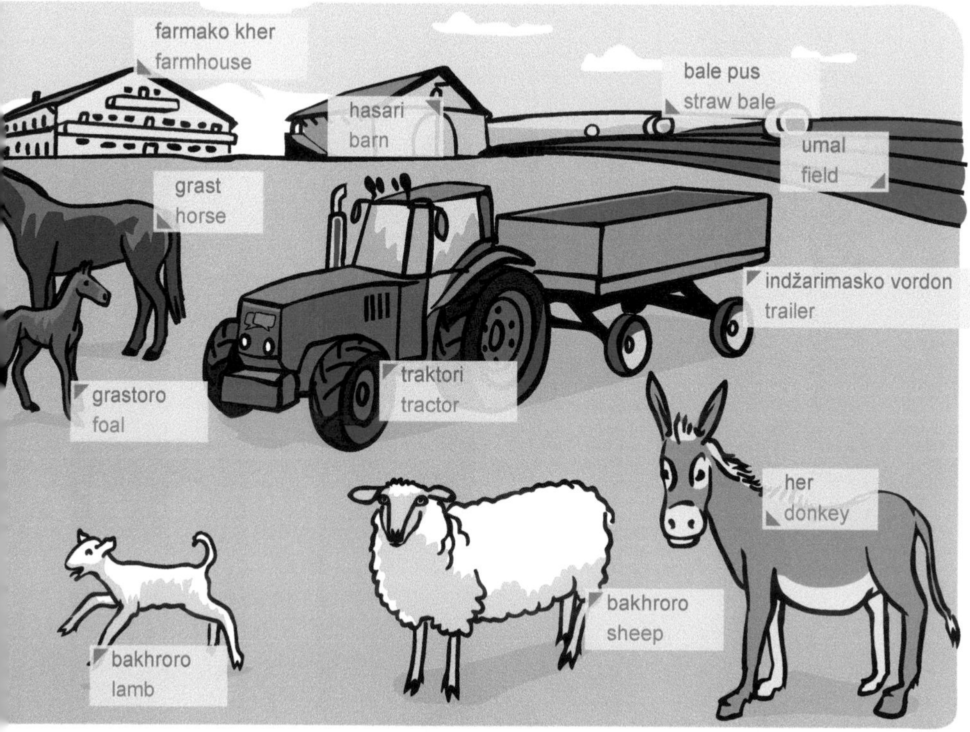

farmako kher
farmhouse
hasari
barn
bale pus
straw bale
umal
field
grast
horse
indžarimasko vordon
trailer
traktori
tractor
grastoro
foal
her
donkey
bakhroro
sheep
bakhroro
lamb

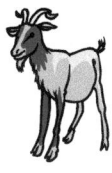

buzno

goat

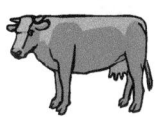

guruvni

cow

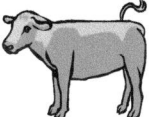

guruvoro

calf

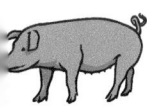

balo

pig

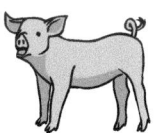

baloro

piglet

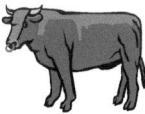

guruv

bull

papin

goose

payka

duck

pilička

chick

khayni

hen

bašno

cock

baro germuso

rat

bilika

cat

germuso

mouse

guruv

ox

džukel

dog

džukelesko kher

doghouse

žardina

garden hose

panyarimaski kanta

watering can

aindžako kidimasko alati

scythe

plugo

plough

srpo

sickle

motika

hoe

aindžaki vilyuška

pitchfork

tover

axe

vordonoro phiravutno

wheelbarrow

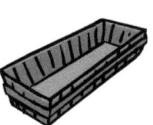

balani

trough

thudeski šiša

milk can

harari

sack

trujalutni

fence

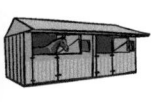

jahri

stable

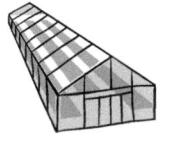

haryalo kher

greenhouse

phuv

soil

seme

seed

gyubre

fertilizer

aindžako kidipe

combine harvester

kidibe aindž

harvest

harmani

harvest

phuvaki phabaj

yams

giv

wheat

soja

soy

kompiri

potato

mumuruzi

corn

šarlagani

rapeseed

emišengo kašt

fruit tree

Kasava

cassava

giveskere javinlukoja

cereals

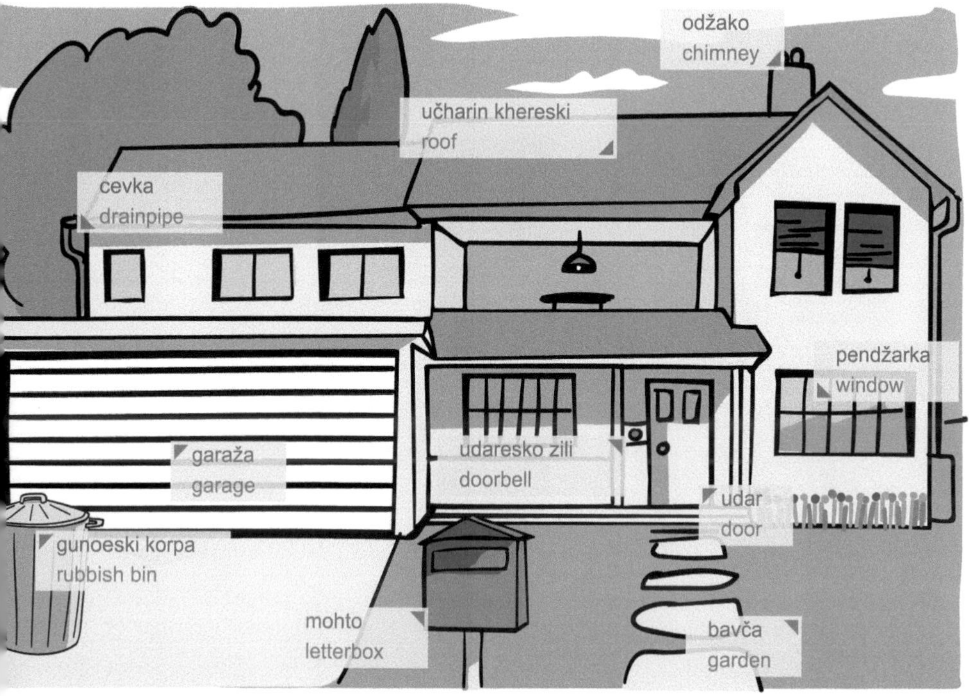

odžako
chimney

učharin khereski
roof

cevka
drainpipe

pendžarka
window

garaža
garage

udaresko zili
doorbell

udar
door

gunoeski korpa
rubbish bin

mohto
letterbox

bavča
garden

ešimaski kamara

living room

banya

bathroom

kujna

kitchen

sovimasko than

bedroom

čhavengi kamara

child's room

than hajbaske rakjako habe

dining room

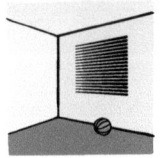

kati
....
floor

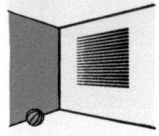

duvari
....
wall

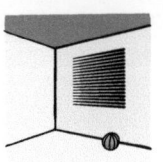

tavano
....
ceiling

špajzi
....
cellar

sauna
....
sauna

terasa
....
balcony

terasa
....
terrace

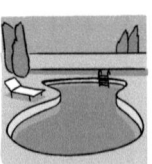

bazeni
....
pool

čar harnyarimaski makina
....
lawn mower

patrin
....
sheet

čaršafia
....
bedspread

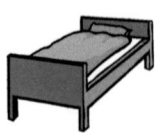

kreveto
....
bed

šulavni
....
broom

korpa
....
bucket

elektrikani phabarin
....
switch

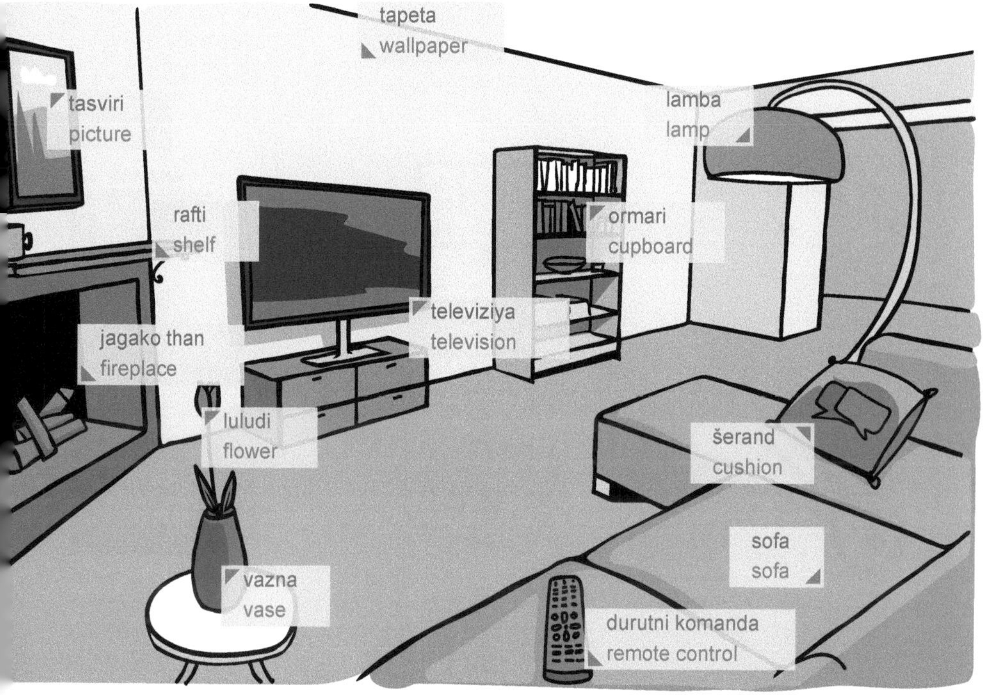

tapeta
wallpaper

tasviri
picture

lamba
lamp

rafti
shelf

ormari
cupboard

jagako than
fireplace

televiziya
television

luludi
flower

šerand
cushion

sofa
sofa

vazna
vase

durutni komanda
remote control

kilimi

carpet

perde

curtain

masa

table

sandaliya

chair

kunajka sandaliya

rocking chair

fotelya

armchair

lil

book

kebe

blanket

dekoraciya

decoration

kašta phabarimaske

firewood

filmi

film

stereo ašunimaske butya

hi-fi equipment

nahtari

key

gazeta

newspaper

frčaja bojakeribe

painting

posteri

poster

radio

radio

hramovimasko bloko

notepad

elektrikani šulavni

hoover

kaktusi

cactus

momoli

candle

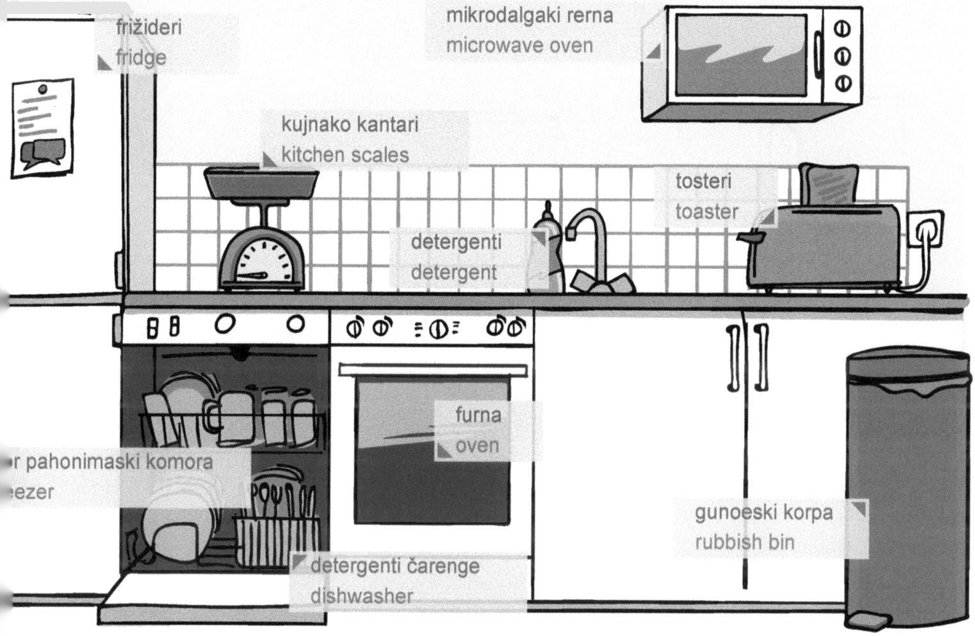

frižderi
fridge

mikrodalgaki rerna
microwave oven

kujnako kantari
kitchen scales

tosteri
toaster

detergenti
detergent

furna
oven

r pahonimaski komora
ezer

gunoeski korpa
rubbish bin

detergenti čarenge
dishwasher

eravimasko than

cooker

čaro

pot

sastrnali tendžera

cast-iron pot

vok cihani

wok / kadai

tava

pan

elektrikano bokali

kettle

tendžera ki para

steamer

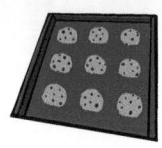

tepsija

baking tray

čare

crockery

bareder fildžano

mug

čaro

bowl

kinakere habaskere kaštore

chopsticks

fioka

ladle

špatula

spatula

vastesko mikseri

whisk

cedimasko čaro

strainer

porizen

sieve

rende

grater

avano

mortar

skara

barbecue

puteribe jag

open fire

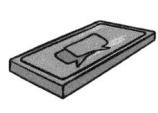

čhinimaski tabla

chopping board

oklagia

rolling pin

puterimasko alati

corkscrew

konzerva

can

konzervako puterutno

can opener

čaresko ikerutno

pot holder

lavabo

sink

frča

brush

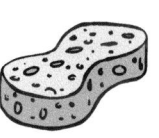

sungeri

sponge

mikseri

blender

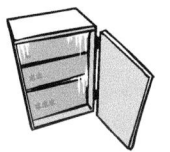

hor pahonimasko frižideri

deep freezer

bebeski šiša

baby bottle

češma

tap

banya

bathroom

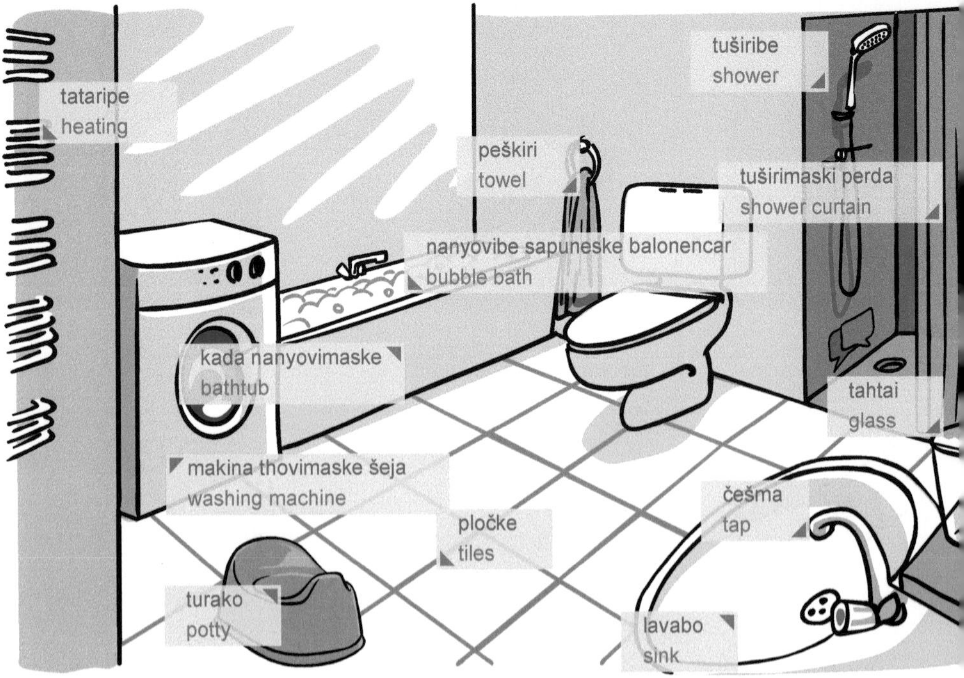

tuširibe
shower
tataripe
heating
peškiri
towel
tuširimaski perda
shower curtain
nanyovibe sapuneske balonencar
bubble bath
kada nanyovimaske
bathtub
tahtai
glass
makina thovimaske šeja
washing machine
češma
tap
pločke
tiles
turako
potty
lavabo
sink

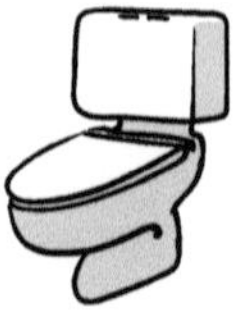

toaleti

toilet

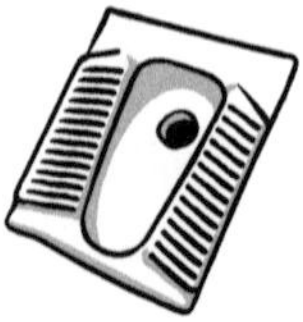

toaleti bešimasa ko pundre

squat toilet

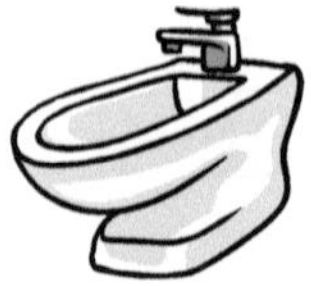

bide

bidet

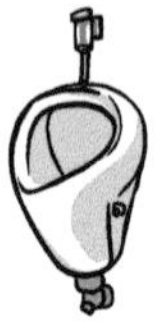

pisoari

urinal

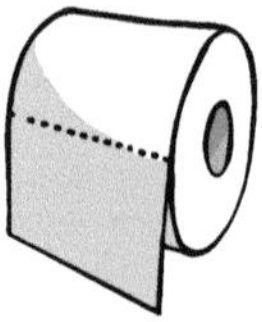

toaletesko lil

toilet paper

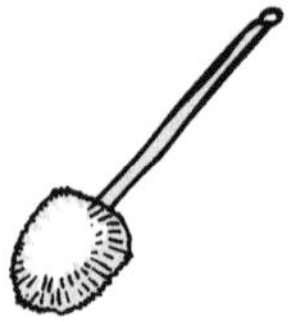

frča toaleteske

toilet brush

nda thovimaski frča

toothbrush

danda thovimaski krema

toothpaste

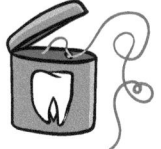

dandesko thav

dental floss

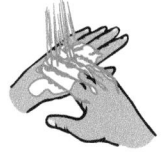

thovibe danda

wash

vasteskoro tuši

handheld shower

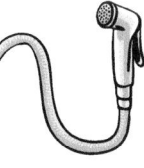

tuši

douche

lavabo

basin

dumeski frča

back brush

sapuni

soap

tuširimasko geli

shower gel

šamponi

shampoo

flanela

flannel

la ćidimaske pani

drain

krema

cream

dezodoransi

deodorant

ajna

mirror

vasteski ajna

hand mirror

žileti moravimaske

razor

moravimaski pena

shaving foam

palal muravimaski krema

aftershave

kanglik

comb

frča

brush

feni balenge

hair dryer

sprej balenge

hairspray

šminka

makeup

karmini

lipstick

oja najenge

nail varnish

pamuko pošom

cotton wool

kata najenge

nail scissors

parfemi

perfume

gono thovimaske

washbag

sandaliya

stool

tereziya

weighing scale

bademantili

bathrobe

gumena kalcunya

rubber gloves

tamponi

tampon

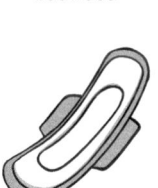

toaletno lil

sanitary towel

hemikano toaleti

chemical toilet

čhavengi kamara

child's room

alarmesko sato
alarm clock
mangli khelutni
cuddly toy
vordonora khelimaske
toy car
tropalka
rattle
bebedžikongo kher
doll's house
bakšiši
present

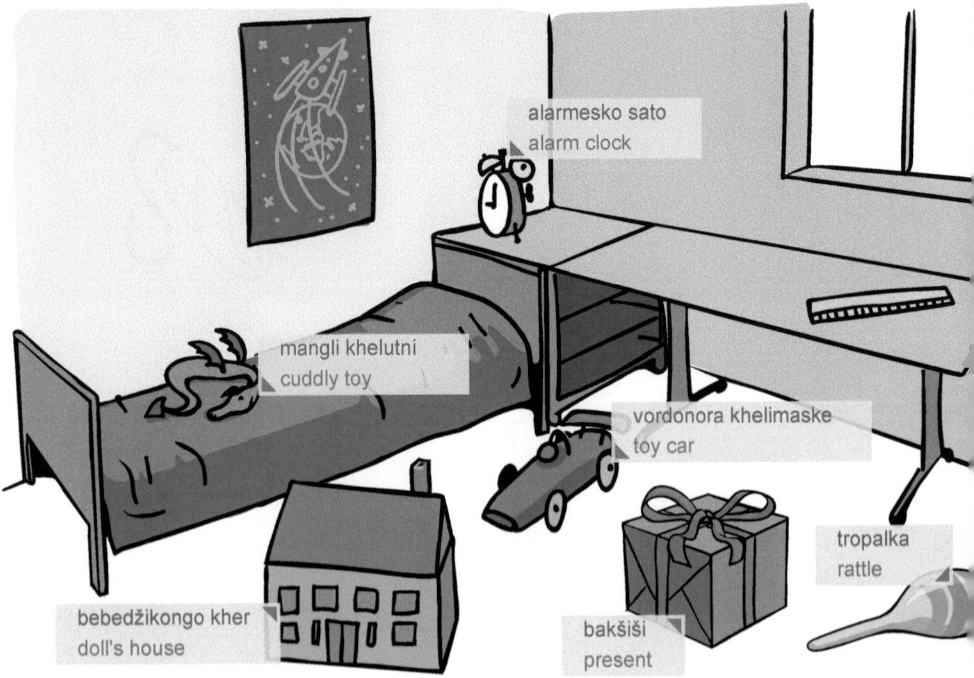

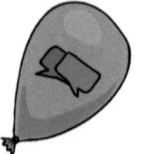

baloni

balloon

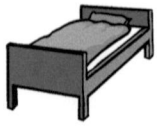

kreveto

bed

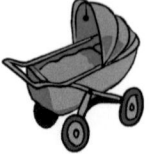

bebengo vordon

pram

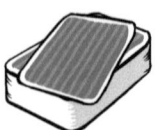

špili karte

deck of cards

ker-rumin khelin

jigsaw

SUPER
MEGA

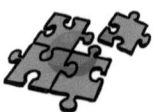

komikano lil

comic

lego kocke

lego bricks

kocke khelimaske

building blocks

akciaki figura

action figure

bodi bebeske

babygrow

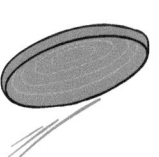

frizbi

frisbee

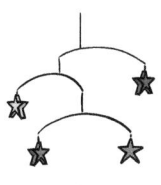

mobile

mobile

nasa khelimaske

board game

zari

dice

pampuri khelimaske

model train set

cucla

dummy

bahlana

party

tasvirengo lil

picture book

topka

ball

bebedžiko

doll

khelibe

play

pošikako than

sandpit

kuna

swing

khelimaske butya

toys

konzola video khelimaske

video game console

triciklo

tricycle

poftaneski ričini

teddy bear

garderoba

wardrobe

šeja
clothing

kalcunya

socks

khuvde kalcunya

stockings

hulahopke

tights

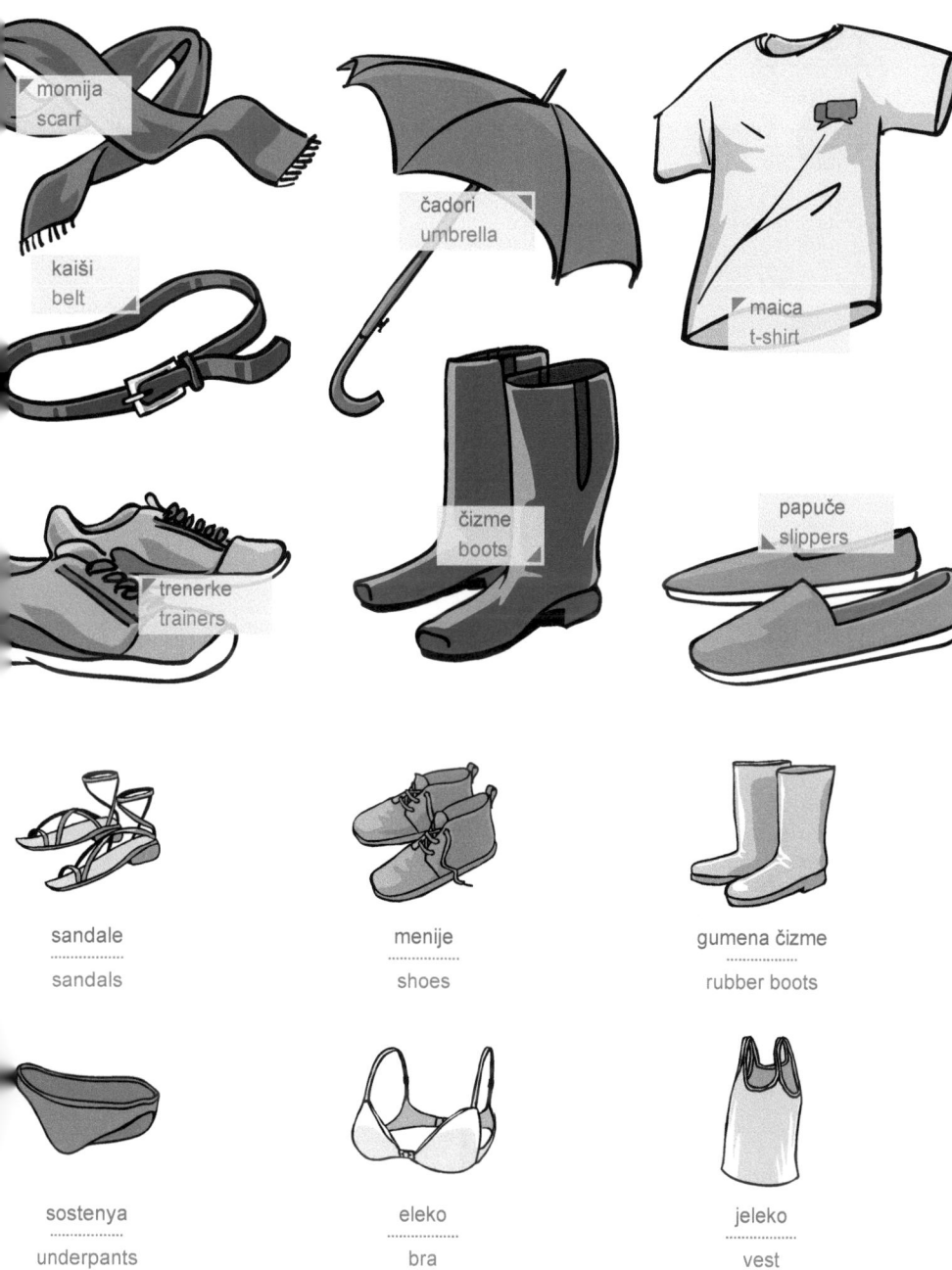

momija
scarf

čadori
umbrella

maica
t-shirt

kaiši
belt

čizme
boots

papuče
slippers

trenerke
trainers

sandale
sandals

menije
shoes

gumena čizme
rubber boots

sostenya
underpants

eleko
bra

jeleko
vest

šeja - clothing

45

bodi
body

pantalonya
trousers

farmerke
jeans

suknya
skirt

bluza
blouse

gat
shirt

puloveri
pullover

dukseri
hoodie

harno kaputi
blazer

džeketi
jacket

kaputi
coat

biršimdesko mantili
raincoat

kostimi
costume

fustano
dress

prandinako fustano
wedding dress

kostumi

suit

rakjako fustano

nightgown

pižame

pyjamas

sari

sari

momija šereske

headscarf

turbani

turban

burka

burqa

kaftani

kaftan

abaya

abaya

ngyovimaske šeja

swimsuit

buxle pantolonya

trunks

harne pantolonya

shorts

orteske trenerke

tracksuit

kecelya

apron

vasteske kalcunya

gloves

kopča

button

gjuzlukya

glasses

belegziya

bracelet

mirikle

necklace

angrustik

ring

čeni

earring

stadik

cap

kaputeski čiviya

coat hanger

stadik

hat

kravata

tie

patenti

zip

kaciga

helmet

dandenge proteze

braces

školaki uniforma

school uniform

uniforma

uniform

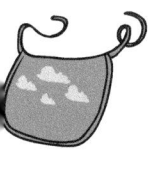

ligarka

bib

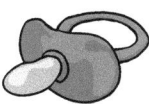

cucla

dummy

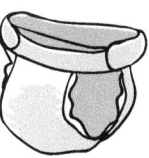

pherno

nappy

ofiso

office

serveri
server
raftija dokumentenca
filing cabinet
printeri
printer
lil
paper
monitori
monitor
mausi
mouse
masa butyake
desk
folderi
folder
tastatura
keyboard
korpa čhudimaske lila
waste-paper basket
kompjuteri
computer
sandaliya
chair

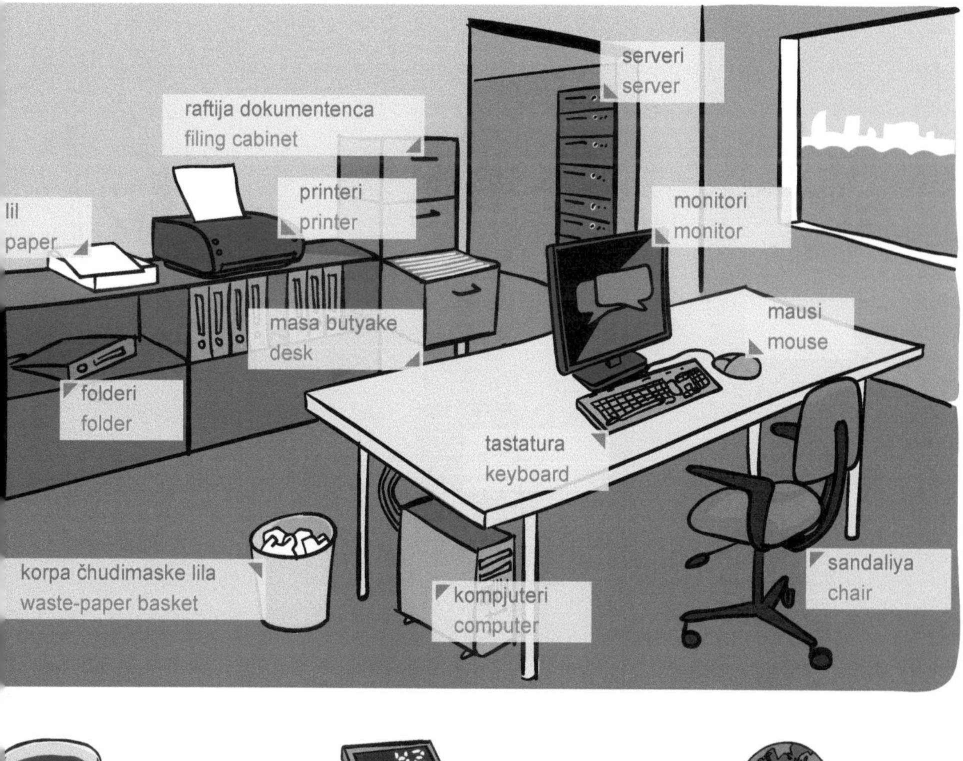

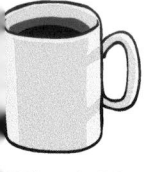

fildžano kafake

coffee mug

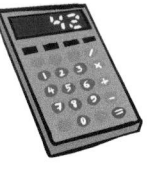

kalkulatori

calculator

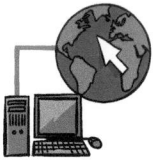

internet

internet

laptop
laptop

lil
letter

mesaži
message

mobilno telefono
mobile

netvorko
network

kopirimaski makina
photocopier

softveri
software

telefono
telephone

štekeri
plug socket

faks makina
fax machine

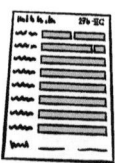

formulari
form

dokumento
document

kinibe

buy

pokinibe

pay

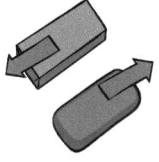

kino-bikinibe

trade

love

money

dolari

dollar

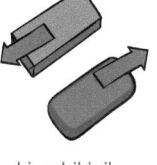

euro

euro

jeni

yen

rublya

rouble

švajcariako franko

Swiss franc

renminbi juan

renminbi yuan

rupija

rupee

lovengo automati

cashpoint

biro baši devize

bureau de change

somnakaj

gold

rup

silver

petroli

oil

energia

energy

fiyati

price

kontrakto

contract

taksa

tax

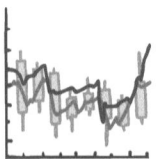

berzaki akcija

stock

butikeribe

work

butyarno

employee

butyako dendutno

employer

fabrika

factory

dukyano

shop

ekonomia - economy

profesie
occupations

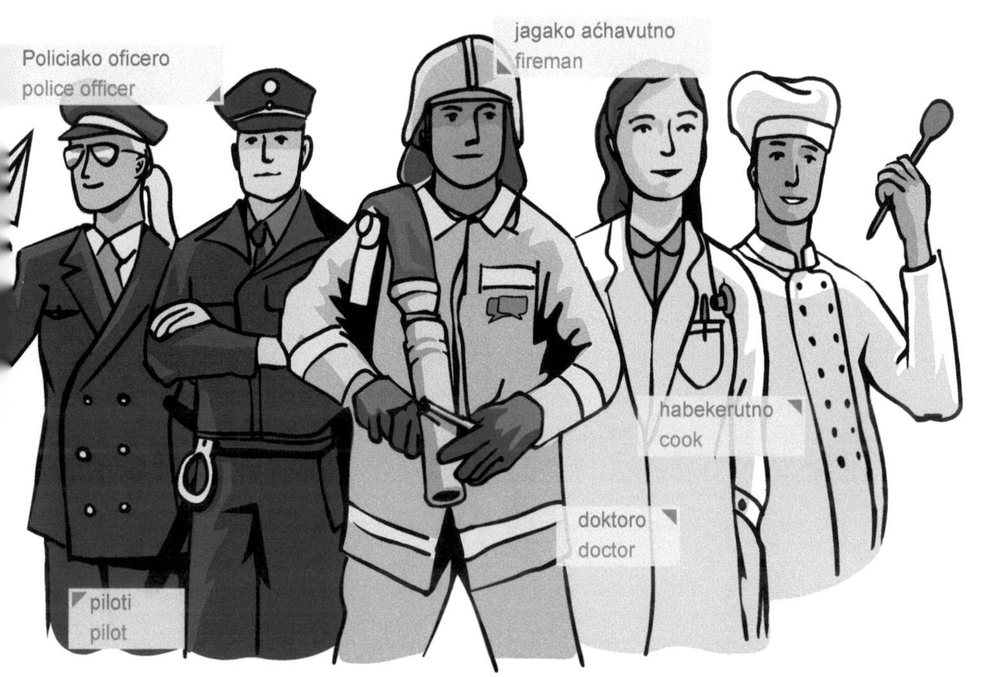

Policiako oficero
police officer
jagako aćhavutno
fireman
habekerutno
cook
doktoro
doctor
piloti
pilot

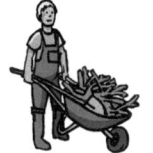

avčako butyarno

gardener

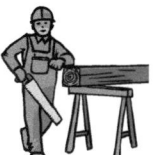

tišleri

carpenter

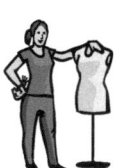

šnajderka

seamstress

krisuno

judge

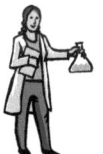

hemičari

chemist

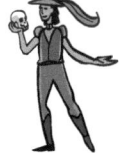

akteri

actor

autobusesko šoferi

bus driver

taksisti

taxi driver

mačhengo astarutno

fisherman

užarutni

cleaning lady

učharinengo kerutno

roofer

kelneri

waiter

avdžija

hunter

tasvirkerutno

painter

furnadžia

baker

elektrikako phirno

electrician

tamirutno

builder

inžinjeri

engineer

kasapi

butcher

panjesko butyarno

plumber

poštari

postman

askeri

soldier

arhitekto

architect

kasieri

cashier

luludyari

florist

frizeri

hairdresser

kondukteri

conductor

mekanisti

mechanic

kapetani

captain

dandengo saslyarno

dentist

gjanalo manuš

scientist

rabini

rabbi

imami

imam

rašaj

monk

rašaj

clergyman

alatia
tools

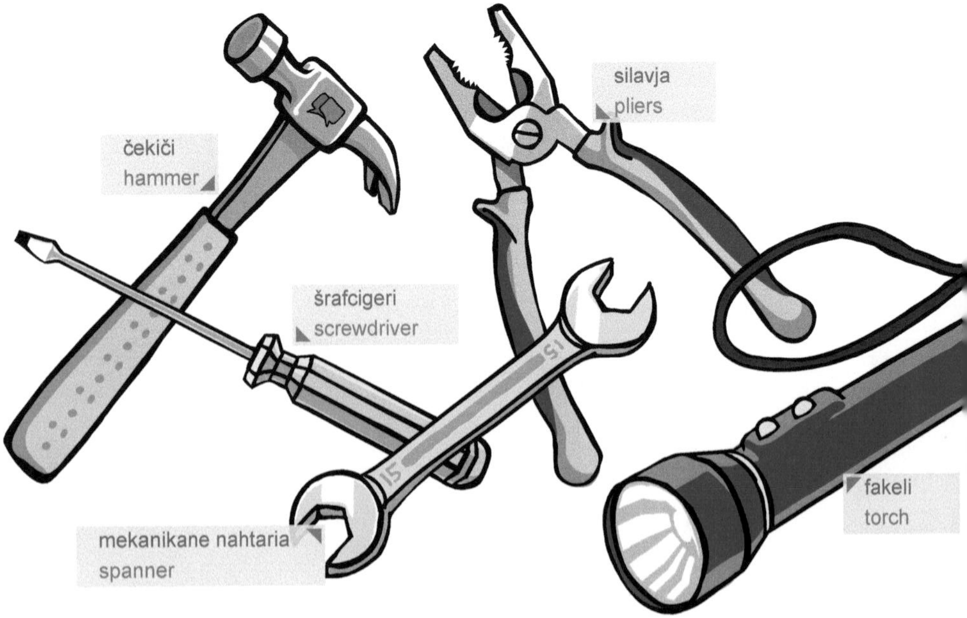

čekiči
hammer
silavja
pliers
šrafcigeri
screwdriver
fakeli
torch
mekanikane nahtaria
spanner

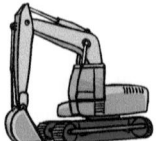

hrandimasko alati

digger

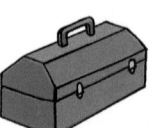

alateski kutia

toolbox

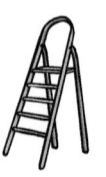

merdeveni

ladder

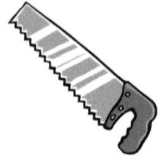

pila

saw

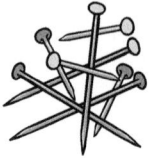

karfa

nails

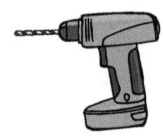

posavin

drill

lačharkeribe
repair

lopata
shovel

Naleti!
Damn!

vatrali
dustpan

lonco bojimaske
paint pot

šrafja
screws

muzikane instrumentia
musical instruments

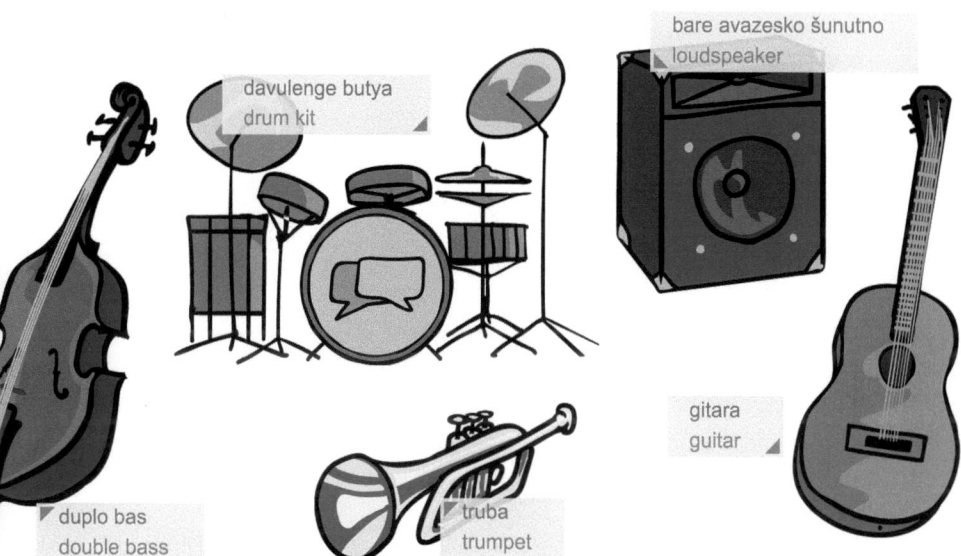

davulenge butya
drum kit

bare avazesko šunutno
loudspeaker

gitara
guitar

duplo bas
double bass

truba
trumpet

piano

piano

kemana

violin

bas

bass

timpani

timpani

davulia

drums

sintisajzeri

keyboard

saksafoni

saxophone

flejta

flute

mikrofoni

microphone

khuvin
entrance

tigari
tiger

kafezi
cage

...ra nakhimaski
...ra

hajvanengo parvaripe
animal feed

panda
panda

hajvania

animals

elefanti

elephant

kenguri

kangaroo

rino

rhino

gorila

gorilla

ričini

bear

kamila

camel

ostriga

ostrich

aslani

lion

majmuni

monkey

flamingo

flamingo

papagali

parrot

polarno ričini

polar bear

pingvini

penguin

ajkula

shark

pauno

peacock

sap

snake

krokodilo

crocodile

zoo arakhutno

zookeeper

foka

seal

jaguari

jaguar

poni

pony

leopardi

leopard

hipo

hippo

žirafa

giraffe

zorale kandžengi paškin

eagle

bali

boar

mačho

fish

želka

turtle

morži

walrus

lumri

fox

gazela

gazelle

Amerikako fudbali
American football

biciklizmo
cycling

tenis
tennis

basketboli
basketball

nangjovibe
swimming

boksi
boxing

hokej ko paho
ice hockey

fudbali
football

badmington
badminton

atletika
athletics

vasteskoboli
handball

skiibe
skiing

polo
polo

aktivitetia

activities

asaibe
laugh
hutibe
jump
deibe angali
hug
phiribe
walk
giljavibe
sing
dikhibe suno
dream
azirikeribe
pray
čumibe
kiss

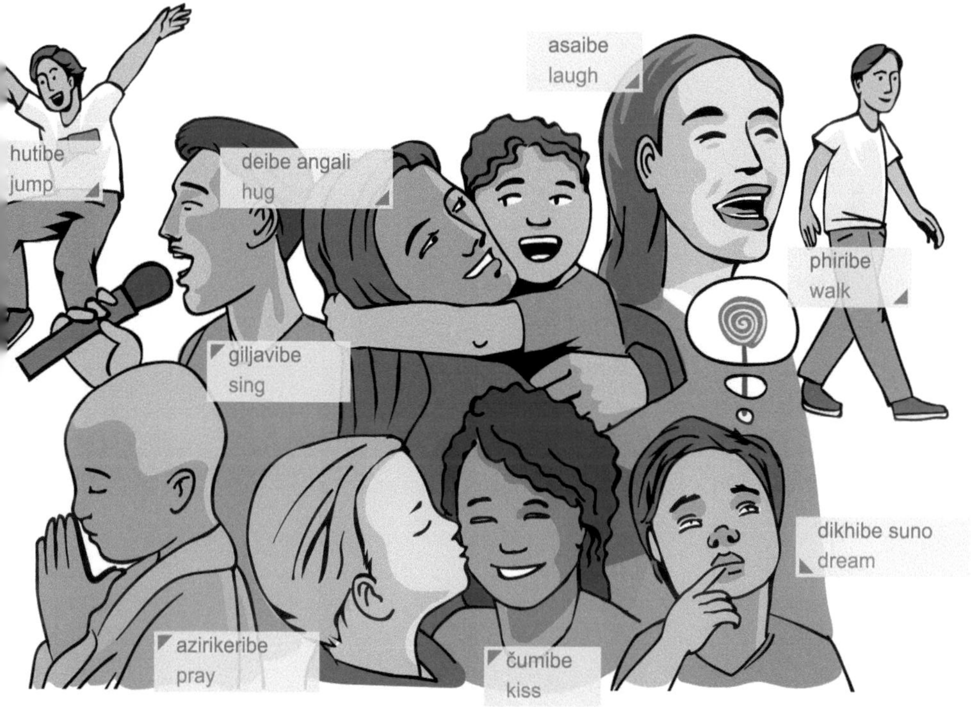

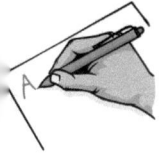

hramovibe

write

čitribe

draw

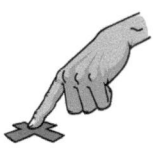

sikavibe

show

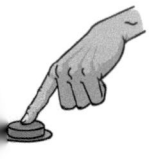

cidljaribe

push

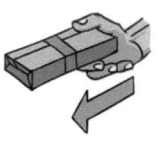

deibe

give

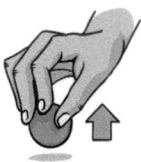

leibe

take

isibe

have

keribe

do

te ovel

be

tergyovibe

stand

prastaibe

run

cidibe

pull

čhudibe

throw

peribe

fall

hovavibe

lie

adžikeribe

wait

phiravibe

carry

bešibe

sit

urjavibe

get dressed

sovibe

sleep

džangavibe

wake up

dikhibe ko

look at

rovibe

cry

čalavibe

stroke

uhlavibr

comb

vakeribe

talk

haljovibe

understand

puč

ask

šunibe

listen

piibe

drink

habe

eat

užaribe

tidy up

kamibe

love

keribe habe

cook

paldibe vordon

drive

urjalibe

fly

aktivitetia - activities

vaporea džaibe

sail

kalkulirin

calculate

drabaribe

read

sikljovibe

learn

butikeribe

work

prandibe

marry

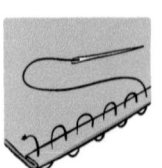

suvibe

sew

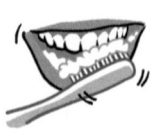

thovibe danda

brush teeth

mudaribe

kill

piibe dahani

smoke

bičhalibe

send

mi
ndmother

papu
grandfather

dat
father

daj
mother

bebe
baby

čhaj
daughter

čhavo
son

misafiri

guest

bibi

aunt

kako

uncle

phral

brother

phen

sister

trupo
body

čekat
forehead
jakh
eye
piko
shoulder
naj
finger
muj
face
vilica
chin
vast
hand
pundro
leg
čuči
breast
musik
arm

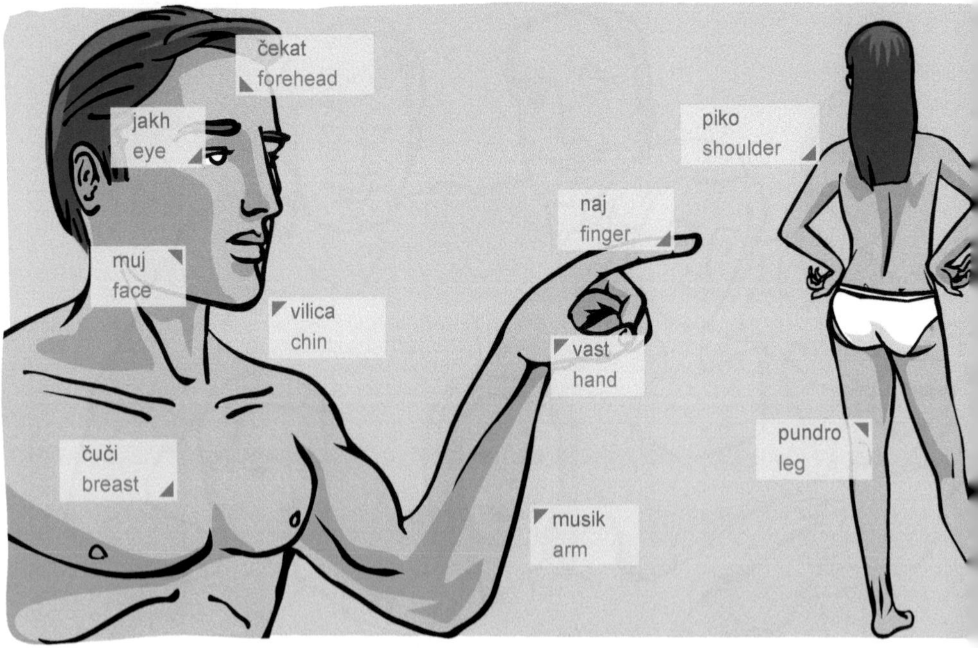

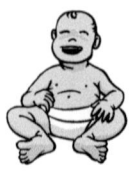

bebe

baby

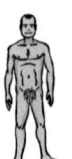

murš

man

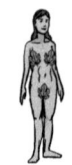

džuvli

woman

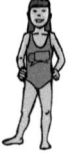

čhaj

girl

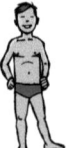

ćhavo

boy

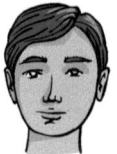

šero

head

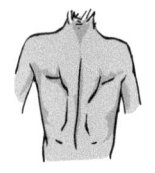

dumo
back

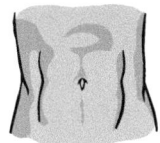

maškar
belly

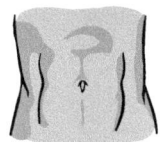

pupko
belly button

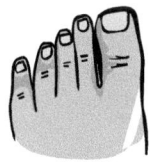

pundrenge naja
toe

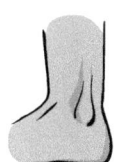

patum
heel

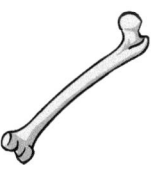

kokalo
bone

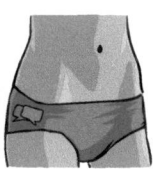

kuko
hip

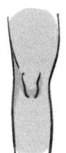

koč
knee

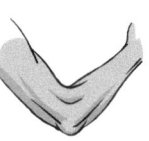

lahci
elbow

nakh
nose

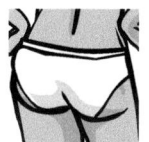

bul
bottom

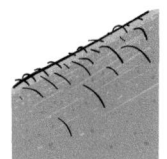

mortik
skin

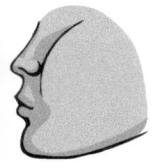

čham
cheek

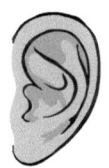

kan
ear

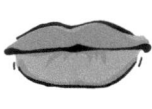

voš
lip

muj

mouth

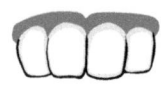

danda

tooth

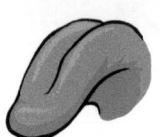

ćhib

tongue

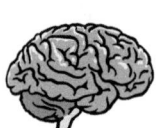

godi

brain

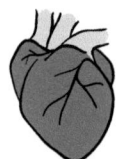

vilo

heart

muskulo

muscle

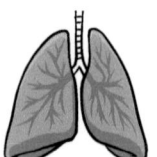

kolin

lung

buko

liver

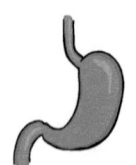

vogi

stomach

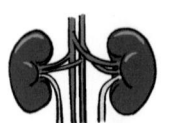

bubrekora

kidneys

seks

sex

kondomi

condom

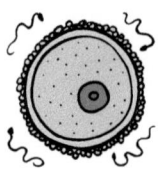

yarengi kletka

ovum

sperma

semen

khamnipe

pregnancy

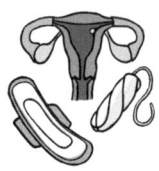

menstruaciya

menstruation

vagina

vagina

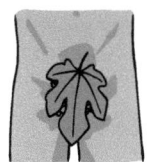

penis

penis

phov

eyebrow

bala

hair

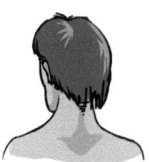

men

neck

hospitalo
hospital

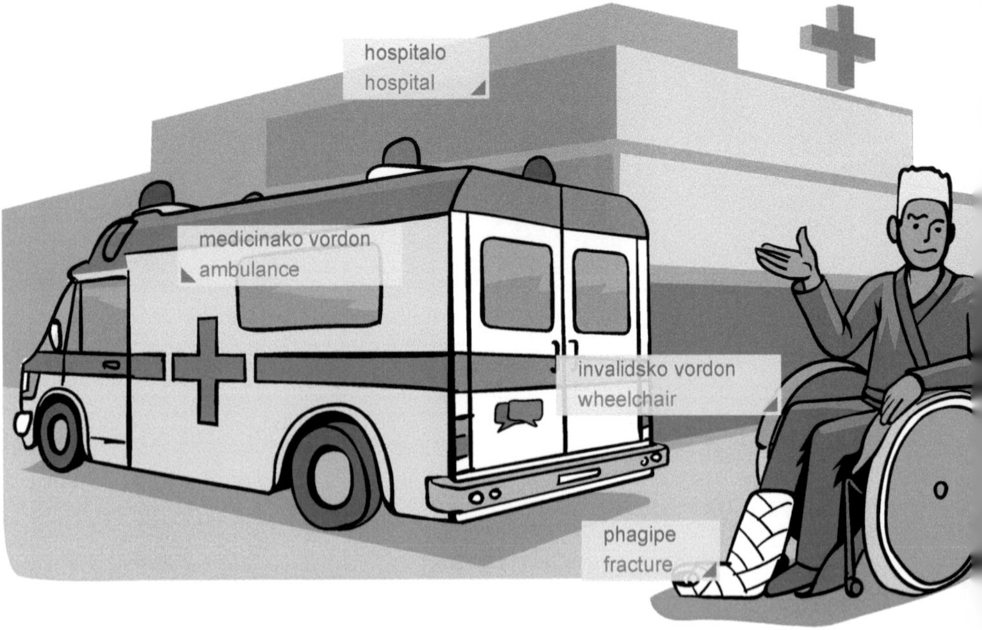

hospitalo
hospital

medicinako vordon
ambulance

invalidsko vordon
wheelchair

phagipe
fracture

doktoro

doctor

sigyarimaski kamara

emergency room

medicinaki phen

nurse

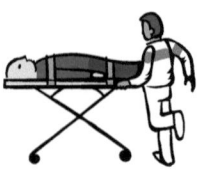

sigyaripen

emergency

ki koma

unconscious

dukh

pain

dukhavipen

injury

ratvaripe

bleeding

infrakto

heart attack

šlog

stroke

alergiya

allergy

khuinibe

cough

tinanipe

fever

gripa

flu

diyarea

diarrhoea

šereski dukh

headache

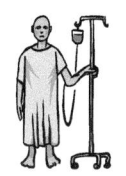

kanceri

cancer

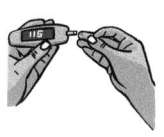

diyabetes

diabetes

operaciya

surgeon

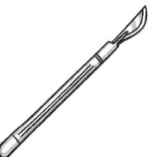

skalperi

scalpel

operaciya

operation

CT

CT

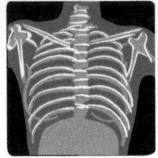

rentgen

x-ray

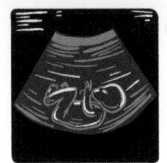

ultra avazo

ultrasound

mujeski maska

face mask

nasvalipe

disease

adžukyarimasko than

waiting room

paterica

crutch

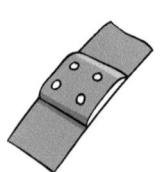

flastero

plaster

phandimaski gaza

bandage

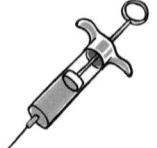

inyekciya

injection

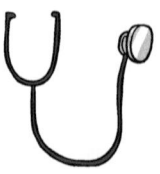

stetoskopo

stethoscope

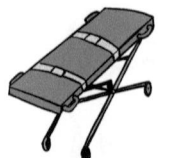

tregero

stretcher

klinicko termometro

clinical thermometer

biyanipe

birth

baro thulipe

overweight

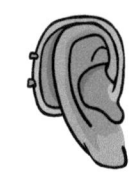

šunimasko aparato

hearing aid

dezinfekciako

disinfectant

infekciya

infection

viruso

virus

HIV / SIDA

HIV / AIDS

medicina

medicine

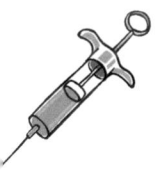

vakcinaciya

vaccination

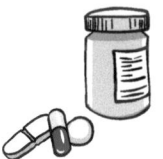

tabletura

tablets

hapi

pill

varimasko akharipe

emergency call

monitori vaš učo pretisak

blood pressure monitor

nasvalo / sasto

ill / healthy

Mažutisar!

Help!

alarmo

alarm

atako

assault

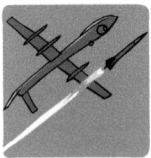

atako

attack

dar buti

danger

sigyarimasko iklyovipen

emergency exit

Bari jag!

Fire!

mamuj jagako aparati

fire extinguisher

bibax

accident

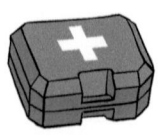

butya avgo ažutimaske

first-aid kit

SOS

SOS

Policia

police

Evropa

Europe

Utarali Amerika

North America

Purabali Amerika

South America

Afrika

Africa

Azija

Asia

Australia

Australia

Atlantiko

Atlantic

Pacifiko

Pacific

Indiako Okeano

Indian Ocean

arktikosko Okeano

Antarctic Ocean

Arktikosko Okeano

Arctic Ocean

Utaralo poli

North Pole

Purabalo poli

South Pole

Antarktiko

Antarctica

phuv

Earth

phuv

land

samudra

sea

džaziri

island

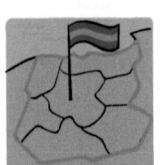

nacija

nation

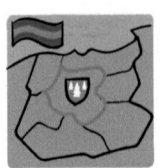

raštra

state

saatosko gendo

clock face

saatoski sikavni

hour hand

dakikongi sikavni

minute hand

darno saatoski sikavin

second hand

Kozom si o saato?

What time is it?

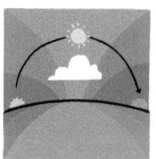

dive

day

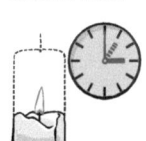

vrama

time

akana

now

digitalno saato

digital watch

dakika

minute

časo

hour

kurko

week

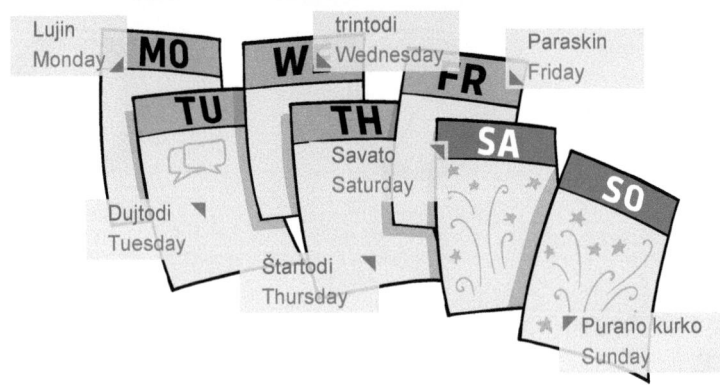

Lujin — Monday
trintodi — Wednesday
Paraskin — Friday
Dujtodi — Tuesday
Savato — Saturday
Štartodi — Thursday
Purano kurko — Sunday

erati

yesterday

avdive

today

tajsa

tomorrow

javin

morning

ekvaš dive

noon

blevel

evening

butyarne divesa

business days

vikend

weekend

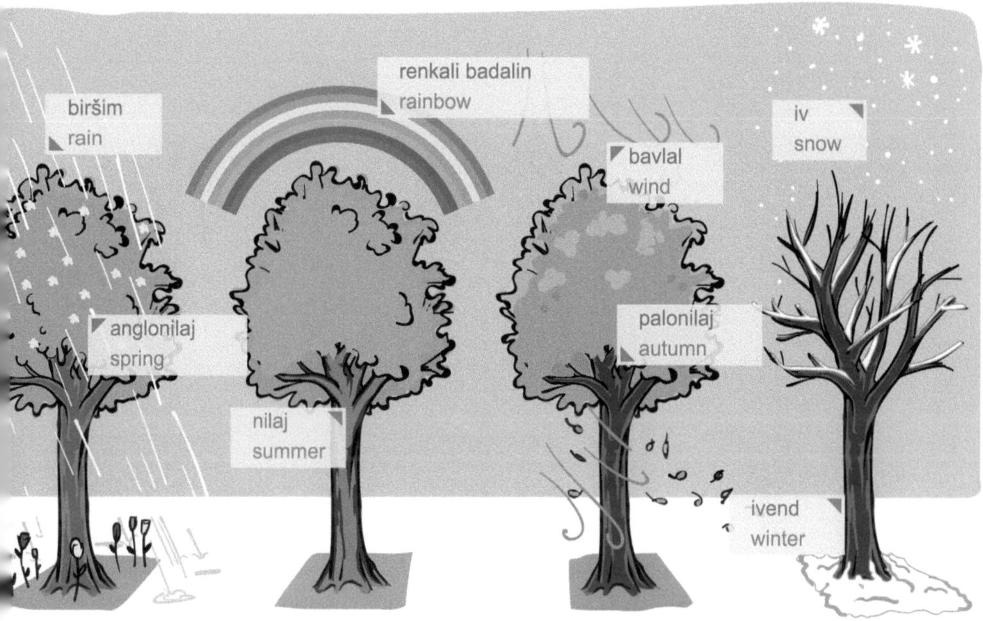

biršim
rain
renkali badalin
rainbow
iv
snow
bavlal
wind
anglonilaj
spring
palonilaj
autumn
nilaj
summer
ivend
winter

4.APRIL 11°
5.APRIL 4°
6.APRIL 13°
7.APRIL 8°
8.APRIL 10°

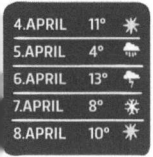

amakoro vakeribe

weather forecast

F C
120 40
90 30
60 20
30 10
0 0
-30 -10
-20

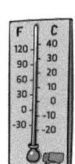

termometro

thermometer

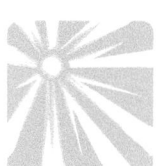

khamalo

sunshine

badal

cloud

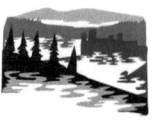

muhi

fog

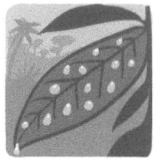

nemlime hava

humidity

šemšekoja

lightning

šemšekosko čalavibe

thunder

bura

storm

kijameti

hail

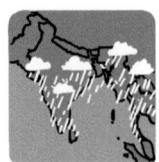

monsuni

monsoon

baro pani

flood

paho

ice

Januaro

January

Februaro

February

Marto

March

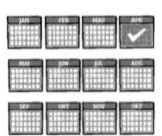

Aprilo

April

Majo

May

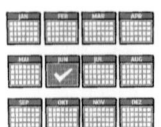

Juno

June

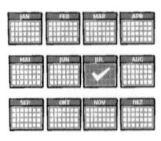

Julo

July

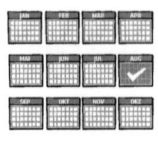

Augusto

August

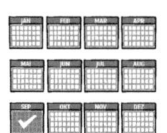

Septembro

September

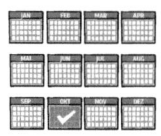

Oktombro

October

Novembro

November

Dekembro

December

rota

circle

kvadrati

square

rektanglo

rectangle

trianglo

triangle

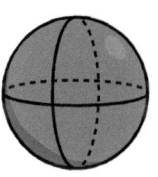

sfera

sphere

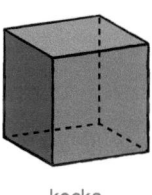

kocka

cube

parni

white

galbeno

yellow

pomarandža

orange

roze

pink

loli

red

lila

purple

vunato

blue

harjali

green

kafeno

brown

kuršumlija

grey

kali

black

but / hari

a lot / a little

holjame / mudro

angry / calm

šuži / bišuži

beautiful / ugly

starto / agor

beginning / end

baro / tikno

big / small

puterde bojako / phanle bojako

bright / dark

phral / phen

brother / sister

užo / melalo

clean / dirty

sahno / bisahno

complete / incomplete

dive / rat

day / night

mulo / dživdo

dead / alive

buvlo / tank

wide / narrow

hala pe / na hala pe

edible / inedible

džungalo / šukar

evil / kind

bare vogjea / bi vogjea

excited / bored

thulo / kišlo

fat / thin

avgo / paluno

first / last

amal / dušmani

friend / enemy

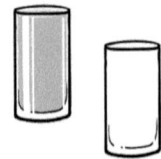

pherdo / čučo

full / empty

zoralo / kovlo

hard / soft

pharo / lokho

heavy / light

bokh / truš

hunger / thirst

nasvalo / sasto

ill / healthy

ilegalno / legalno

illegal / legal

godyaver / bigodyako

intelligent / stupid

bajan / dahin

left / right

paše / dur

near / far

nevo / purano

new / used

khanči / vareso

nothing / something

phuro / terno

old / young

habardo / ačhavdo

on / off

puterdo / phanlo

open / closed

mudro / bare avazeskoro

quiet / loud

barvalo / čorolo

rich / poor

čačutno / došalo

right / wrong

zoralo / kovlo

rough / smooth

mazuni / lošalo

sad / happy

skurto / lungo

short / long

pohari / sigate

slow / fast

sapano / šuko

wet / dry

tato / šudro

warm / cool

mareba / sansari

war / peace

0

zero

zero

1

jek

one

2

duj

two

3

trin

three

4

štar

four

5

panč

five

6

šov

six

7

efta

seven

8

ohto

eight

9

enja

nine

10

deš

ten

11

dešujek

eleven

12
dešuduj

twelve

13
dešutrin

thirteen

14
dešuštar

fourteen

15
dešupanč

fifteen

16
dešušov

sixteen

17
dešefta

seventeen

18
dešohto

eighteen

19
dešenja

nineteen

20
biš

twenty

100
šel

hundred

1.000
milja

thousand

1.000.000
milioni

million

Anglicko

English

Americko Anglicko

American English

Kinesko Mandarinsko

Chinese Mandarin

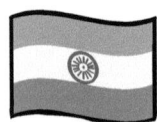

Indisko

Hindi

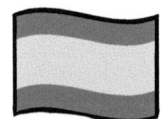

Špansko

Spanish

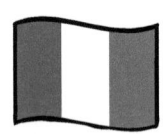

Francusko

French

Arapsko

Arabic

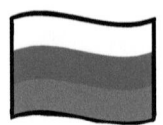

Rusko

Russian

Portugalsko

Portuguese

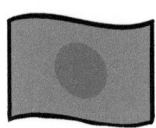

Bengalsko

Bengali

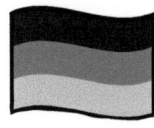

Nemicko

German

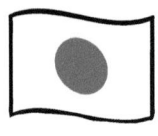

Japansko

Japanese

thaj

I

tu

you

ov / oj

he / she / it

amen

we

tumen

you

ola

they

ko?

who?

so?

what?

sar?

how?

kote?

where?

kana?

when?

anav

name

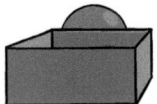

palal

behind

andre

in

anglal o

in front of

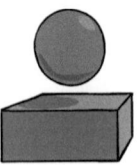

upral

over

an

on

telal

under

trujal

beside

maškaral

between

than

place